Summary a

of

Factfulness: Ten Reasons We're Wrong About the World – And Why Things Are Better Than You Think

by

Hans Rosling

Nosco Publishing

Note to readers:

This is an unofficial summary and analysis of Hans Rosling's *Factfulness: Ten Reasons We're Wrong About the World – And Why Things Are Better Than You Think* designed to enrich your reading experience.

Attention: Our Gift to You

As a way of thanking you for purchasing *this* book, we would like to give you another book as a gift: *Stoicism: The Art of Living a Modern Stoic and Happy Life Now.*

If you would like a copy, please visit:

http://NoscoPublishing.com/offer/

Regards,

Nosco Publishing

Table of Contents

BOOK SUMMARY OVERVIEW

Most of us have skewed conceptions of the world around us and live according to basic tenents and beliefs that may not be true. Author Hans Rosling seeks to turn the tides on outdated facts that many of us still hold. For instance, for most of human history the larger portion of the global population lived on the brink of death. However, is this still the case in the early 21th century?

Hans Rosling is joined by his son Ola Rosling and his son's wife Anna Rosling Rönnlund. The Rosling authors provide a new data set from which a more up to date and accurate view of the global population and their well-being may be developed. In the past, there was such a massive gap between the poor and the wealthy that, if you were born poor, was completely insurmountable. The fundamental goal of *Factfulness: Ten Reasons We're Wrong About the World – And Why Things Are Better Than You Think* is to show that this understanding about poverty and wealth no longer applies to most of modern society.

The term "most" itself is discussed and readers are cautioned on ingesting this term whole. Rather, information seekers must work to find out what specific percentages are behind this label of "most." The book expresses the overuse of generalizations that can lead to inaccurate or incomplete information. This effect can easily result in costly mistakes that may have easily been avoided had better numbers been sought. Fifty-one percent and ninety-six percent are both majorities. Yet, they offer drastic differences in their meanings for large company investments and world health concerns.

Investment companies miss a huge market if numbers are not correctly understood. World leaders miss opportunities to better provide for their constituents when inaccurate percentages are used. Safety, health, and the wellbeing of many are greatly missed when false perceptions lead to treatment of situations that may turn out to be mild compared to greater risks that are not readily seen.

Numbers alone do not tell the whole story. They help us get where we need to go in terms of communicating the parameters of a possible situation. However, a simple look in the right place at the right time may offer just what is needed to gauge the health of communities on the local level. Leaders need to ensure that the time is taken to view government decisions in light of current information that is based on recent data – not information that may have been presented to them decades ago.

The Roslings seek to provide the public with a more accurate perspective of global populations and the risks and dangers that may be encountered. As a physician, Hans Rosling is able to travel to remote parts of the globe and assist in a number of unique and trying medical situations. He tells those stories in a relatable, yet informative manner. Readers may easily be drawn to the realities and honesties of the experiences that Hans uses to portray what he feels is important to understand about international matters today. He shares his deepest thoughts and emotions in a way that allows the reader to laugh with him and still somehow find a new level of human fortitude and motivation.

Methods for attaining the most accurate view of a situation are included for each of the 13 questions that are discussed. The book concludes with a challenge for the reader to consider all that was learned by having been exposed to the information given. Readers are encouraged to search for the truth in each situation that is encountered in life. The need to update information is imperative for maintaining an accurate view of almost any scenario that involves matters of changes in population, global weather and temperature concerns, health matters, and poverty concerns.

The authors add a bit of fun to the challenge stating that those who have received a degree from a university in the past need to be sent updated information noting that what may have been learned decades ago is no longer relevant. Readers are provoked to remain in a continuing education mindset for the purpose of promoting long-term health and wellness of all global inhabitants.

CHAPTER BY CHAPTER ANALYSIS

Introduction

Hans Rosling's desire to help global citizens better understand the world in its true form takes the reader through an interesting path in *Factfulness: Ten Reasons We're Wrong About the World – And Why Things Are Better Than You Think*. Thirteen questions are presented that relate to birth, deaths, education, health, and poverty vs. wealth as they occur in the populations of nations across the globe. The reader is given multiple choice options and is directed to answer according to his or her current knowledge. These questions and their answers are explained in detail throughout the book and the reader is prompted to consider the information in a manner that allows them to *see the truth* of a situation and act upon it fairly.

The Gap Instinct

The perspective of individuals who grew up in decades past will likely have an outdated view of the status of the world's population and its impact on local societies. Facts and principles that were taught 20, 30, 40, and 50 years ago do not accurately reflect the facts of the world in the early 21th century. Yet, many educated adults still hold onto the information they were given during their school days decades ago. The "Gap Instinct" is the natural inclination to apply this outdated data to the world today.

Due to old information, certain views and perceptions can be misleading and result in improper proportions when impactful decisions about the world must be made. The terms "developed" and "developing" that have long been used to describe the state of a nation or community no longer offer the best representation of how societies function worldwide. It is noted that 75% of people live in middle-income countries. The enormous gap that once separated the poor from the wealthy no longer exists. What now may be found is that much of the world's families have begun to find their way to clean water, education, and vaccinations.

These basic, relatively inexpensive, community options have offered the greatest vehicles for improvement on the local level – worldwide. The key to note here is that this began to occur throughout the world several decades ago. Enough time has now passed that quite a few of these small, once poverty-ridden, communities have been able to work their way to a greater life than many of them once experienced. The result is that grandparents living today are watching their grandchild live in such a way that they never dreamed might be possible.

The authors present a four-level system that displays a more accurate layout of how modern society is aligned in communities and nations. These four levels offer a more detailed representation of how modern populations have changed over the last 200+ years of history.

This information is presented to the reader with a "video game" theme. Readers are encouraged to read through the information regarding each level as though they must earn the money needed to move from level to level as they read. Pictorial images are provided to help the reader grasp what is available in the lives of the populations represented at each of the levels.

- **Level 1** represents a family that begins at $1 per day. Transportation is only available by one's own feet. Water is obtained by mud hole (usually dirty) and carried over long distances daily. Firewood must be gathered to cook the same type of porridge daily – if that porridge is available. In order to proceed to Level 2, more than $2 per day must be earned. Approximately 1 billion people are considered Level 1 today.

- **Level 2** welcomes families that earn between $2 and $8 dollars daily. You can now buy a bike to help transport water, some much-needed food, and possibly sandals for your children. A small gas stove purchase frees up some time. Your children may now attend school instead of finding and carrying wood for cooking purposes. Approximately 3 billion people currently live on Level 2.

- **Level 3** represents families that earn between $9 and $31 per day. Your work has not been light, but you now have enough money to run a line for cold water. This saves you even more time per day, allowing you to continue to increase your productivity for a better lifestyle. You are able to save enough funds to purchase a refrigerator to store more food types. You eventually buy a motorbike and begin working further away, earning even more money per day. The family is eventually able to take a short one-day vacation. Approximately 2 billion people reside in a Level 3 environment.

- **Level 4** shows families that earn $32 or more per day. It wasn't easy but your family, perhaps over the course of a generation or two has moved from Level 1 to Level 4. Controlling the temperature of the water you use at home is an option that you now have. The possibilities for a car, eating out on occasion, and upper-level education are likely something that will be experienced by individuals living on

Level 5 The text notes that readers of *Factfulness: Ten Reasons We're Wrong About the World – And Why Things Are Better Than You Think* are likely already familiar with Level 4 because they live on it. Having the time and resources to even read the book shows that the reader has the resources and lifestyle of someone living in Level 4. The authors note that Level 4 dwellers may not feel that $3 a day is much and will often have a difficult time grasping the concepts of surviving on Level 1.

The authors note that the human history began with all of mankind on Level 1. Throughout the course of life on earth, man has survived in quite rudimentary settings. Children often did not survive to adulthood. It has only been in the last few centuries that such dramatic improvements have happened – especially in rapid sequencing. Even "just 200 years ago, 85 percent of the world population was still on Level 1, in extreme poverty." Changes to daily environments in which many people now find themselves have come in such rapid fashion that in a single lifetime some older generations have experienced life on several of the levels. Many individuals have watched as their parents began on Level 1 and then later their grandchildren grow up on Levels 3 or 4.

The Negativity Instinct

The world is falling apart faster and faster. At least that is the concept that many individuals hold onto as they form perceptions about the earth and the people who live upon it. The Rosling authors seek to debunk this misconception through a myriad of surveys and personal interviews with folks from all walks of life.

As technology has progressed, the possibilities for gaining information regarding the current state of matters in any regard has changed drastically. This means that a good portion of the world has the option to easily access near each and every catastrophe that happens worldwide. By perception, this spurs an increased sense of doom. Earthquakes, fires, murders, terror attacks, and the like are taking place all over that globe – but not every one of them is happening in each person's backyard by the day. Rather, we bring these events into our homes from all over the world through modern traditional and social media.

It does not make for an eye-catching breaking news story to say that 900 school children attended school without any major deaths, injuries, or health hazards. That is what we expect. Therefore, when a day that is as to be expected occurs, journalists are not likely to grab up that day's school events for the 5 o'clock news hour.

Survey data shows that a good portion of the world's population believes that the world is getting worse. The authors explain that poverty rates have plummeted in the last 200 years. Life expectancy has also jumped from approximately 30 to 70 years for many countries in the last 200. The overall health and wealth that citizens of many countries experience has improved dramatically, overall.

In fact, countries have a found themselves with billions of people – once on Level 1 – now living in Level 2 and 3 societies. The interesting thing that the authors highlight in this chapter is that much of these changes have taken place without the eyes of those already on Level 4. These advancements took place without Level 4 citizens even noticing.

The facts given represent a world full of improvements and betterment. Yes, many horrific matters still must be considered. The book, in no way, speaks to minimize the terrible and heart-wrenching problems that individuals of the globe must still endure. However, the rate in which humans are able to prevent, avoid, and eliminate disease and basic sanitary health hazards remains one of several crucial advancements to society.

Add to this the ability to more accurately determine when hurricanes, tornadoes, or earthquakes may threaten human lives and there just another tool in our favor for survival. The book seeks to bring to mind how such advancements have benefited the approximately seven billion residents of the globe for a better life while on it.

The Straight Line Instinct

What goes up will always go up right? Well maybe. Here the authors work to help the reader understand that just because the population of the globe was once increasing with great speed, does not mean that it will always continue to do so. Rather, as the overall health and wellness of the global population has increased, the once great need to have lots of children has decreased.

The **Gapminder Foundation**[1] is an organization that was originated by the Rosling authors for the purpose of helping global citizens have better access to accurate and up to date information. The Foundation's mission is "to fight devastating ignorance with a fact-based worldview."

In a society where children die regularly from disease, hunger, and other misfortunes, families often need to have more than five in order to hopefully have at least two survive past the age of five and on into adulthood. As mothers become more educated on how to help their children survive, the need to have many children decreases. Education for the benefit of the health of humans goes a long, long way toward stabilizing – or plateauing – of the global population.

---

[1] https://www.gapminder.org/

The authors explain that it is a "mega misconception that 'the world is just increasing and increasing.'" While it is true that data will sometimes present a doubling effect, as with the Ebola Outbreak in which more than 11,000 people died, not all matters of global population are "just" increasing leaving the globe to house more and more lives. Rather, we can now look at the changes that include a longer life expectancy but fewer lives, essentially, longer, better, fewer lives from birth onward. According to the data presented in the book, the human population is expected to plateau around the year 2100. Meaning that the effects of living on Levels 2 and 3 (instead of Level 1) have already begun to take effect on the lives of those who will birth generations to come. According to the text, United Nations experts predict that 2 billion children between the ages of 0 and 14 will be alive in the year 2100.

Tomorrow's grandchildren are predicted to birth fewer children. This will mean that fewer cycles of birth and death will take place than will be expected if people continue to have lots of children in hopes of having a few survive into adulthood. Generations of people are now living to see their children's grandchildren. This is a groundbreaking thing for a collection of people who once hoped to see their own children survive past the age of five.

Yes, the human population has grown rapidly in the course of history. This does not mean that the same pattern is to be continued in the years to come. One chart provided in the text notes that the human population stayed roughly the same (5 million people) until around 1800. Then we began to see a rapid growth in the worldwide population. This growth happened so rapidly that concerns began to arise regarding how the earth would possibly withstand so many new lives. Such concerns are now met with updated facts that the earth's capacity to house the growing human population may now be put to rest.

Now we may seek to provide a healthier, safer way of life for the stabilizing human population. In short, the average mother worldwide now gives birth to 2.5 children who have a much greater chance to grow to have their own children while their mother is still living. In 1948 the number of children born to mothers worldwide was 5. This is a dramatic drop in a short amount of time. It is in direct reflection to an increase in health and the ability to keep babies alive longer.

The Fear Instinct

Hans Rosling does it again! His ability to catch the reader's interest through the events of his life is not lost even this far into the book. Hans tells of a story in his early days as a physician in which he let fear take over his decision-making skills. Instead of pausing to assess the situation, he quickly concludes that the man on the table before him is a foreign soldier about to die from a wound that Hans just cannot seem to find. A more seasoned head nurse joins him and scolds his actions as he is about to cut into an expensive flight suit the man is wearing. She tells him to remove his foot from the life jacket under it because he has just spilled its red dye all over the floor.

Humbled, Hans uses this experience to help readers understand the importance of properly gathering information in order to form our perspectives. When we insist on holding onto only a single perspective without the possibility of adding to what we currently know – or altering it completely – we risk causing harm to ourselves and others around us. Fears drive us in the moment of life to make choices that we might not otherwise make only to later discover how silly our narrow view left us.

In today's world, the media plays a large role in creating an increased level of fear. The authors do not say that we should never consider anything that the news sources offer. Yet, filtering information in a way that allows us to more correctly view the information presented is recommended. If numbers are given, always look for a comparison. Lone numbers create false representations of reality. If 100 people died, is that number higher or lower than in years past? Numbers must be used appropriately in order to determine if progress has been made or if a problem has begun to develop that needs attention in some way.

It is expected that the media will not change much in the way it seeks to get the public's attention. News stories that offer bland and normal life events do not catch the attention of anyone. It is no secret that media producers thrive on the basic instinct of human fear and we offer them plenty of fodder as a species. The authors note that three human fears helped us survive. Fears of physical harm, captivity, and contamination have helped to keep us alive for generations. Journalists who wish to keep their jobs will continue to provide dramatic and eye-catching stories and we, as the consumers of media, must consider the context in which these stories are told and hold their information accordingly.

A distinction is made for individuals on Levels 1 and 2 regarding the realities of such fears that may still be faced in their communities. Dangers are different when medical care is not available and no one has trained your leaders on the realities of poison due to a change in food preparation. Notably, Hans tells of a midwife whose wish was to have a flashlight in order to see the snakes when she must travel in the dark to assist with the birth of a child. The dangers are very different when income levels are considered.

It is noted that at this juncture in history, "almost every aspect of global development" has data available for review. Even in the midst of our best efforts we, as humans, still often allow our instincts for survival to overtake our rational thinking and create fear within us. This does not help us make helpful decisions for our families or communities and we must fight the urge to retain only a single perspective on any situation that life brings to us. It is suggested that fear of great danger for individuals on Levels 3 and 4 may cause more harm than is needed since there already exists protection from most dangers.

Natural disasters still bring death to large numbers of people worldwide, however, the numbers show that due to better buildings, warning systems, and education on Levels 2, 3, and 4 we have begun to minimize deaths that may occur as a result of natural disasters. All of the levels still experience multiple deaths due to any one event but many are able to prepare or escape the danger before it strikes. When natural disasters do strike, emergency response teams are often called in from other parts of the globe to help locate survivors, provide short-term food and water options, and even start the process of restoration.

These resources do not come from poverty-stricken communities. "Level 4 taxpayers" provide such resources. The authors note the irony of the fact that media presentations do not readily permit Level 4 taxpayers to see the results of their payments. Instead, it is much more attention getting to provoke human instinct of fear and portray each event as the worst the world has ever seen. In fact, the event may have been very bad with many deaths – but still better than it might have been if modern considerations had not been available.

The authors ask if readers will be able to recall such information and form a more clear perspective as they observe their next news media story. Will you try to consider how the events of that story compare in relation to the everyday events of individuals living on Level 1?

Plane crashes, radioactivity, and DDT have all once placed fear into the lives of those who lived at the time of their integration into society. Planes became better and safer but humans still feared them for many years after the decline in crashes took place. Radioactivity has its harmful properties that must be considered and yet, its dangers are still largely misunderstood by those who grew up in the nuclear age. DDT began its days under speculation. It's use sparked a fear of chemicals that may prevent accurate information regarding its benefits for preventing disease when used properly.

The authors seek to help the public understand the differences between frightening and dangerous. A perceived risk may or may not become a potential danger in reality. It is beneficial for us to understand the difference and be able to recognize each as we encounter them. Readers are encouraged to "get calm before you carry on."

The instinct to flee from the presence of danger has helped humans to survive for many generations – as it does for much of the rest of earth's creatures. We encounter something that may be harmful to us or our children and we kill it, run from it, or escape it in some manner. Hurricanes, plagues, and cars in the street all bring us the potential to encounter danger. As a human society, we work to minimize the risks that may come our way.

Our reactive natures have kept us alive as a species through tens of thousands of years that brought new types of danger quite often. Families living on Level 1 may still often encounter a number of dangers that may not be quite as prevalent in a country that has the ability to move up a level. Families living on Level 4 will not only have greater benefit from governmental emergency recovery systems, but they will also be more likely to be able to take advantage of preventative services.

For example, weather alert systems help to prevent casualties in societies where they have been made available. Vaccines are another resource that helps us to prevent widespread death and disease. Illness may still strike a community or a nation and must be dealt with accordingly. The option to provide the human body with advanced care for such diseases *prior to exposure* has dramatically affected our ability to live in a world where illnesses themselves may still be found. Not only does this work to keep individuals alive, it helps to prevent the rapid spread of disease.

In situations where vaccines have not been developed, antibiotics can play a role in the well-being of individuals. However, this is not meant to be the solution to everything. Prevention through education, vaccination, and proper food and waste handling serve as the vanguard for the health and wellness of people in all income levels.

The world can be a scary place but it can often seem much scarier than it is. The authors wish for readers to have a better and more accurate understanding of what dangers may be encountered as residents of a more advanced global community. Dangers that exist on one continent may not have a direct impact on whether or not a person on another continent will remain safe.

This does not mean that those in danger should not receive assistance. Rather than seeing a tornado shelter when a storm is thousands of miles away, we can pay more direct attention to any dangers that reside closer to us, then helping to improve storm alert systems and the science behind them would seem to be a more relevant act than running scared underground when the current storm is passing on another continent.

The authors work to help readers better understand what dangers are real and relevant in modern society but our perception of their dominance is outdated and, thus, inaccurate. The health and safety of communities on one continent may or may not be impacted by a natural disaster happening on another. Compassion is not left out. We can still work to improve the situation for our global neighbors and it must be understood that each and every disease and natural disaster that residents of the earth encounter will not have a direct impact on each human.

Panic and fear do not help us make beneficial decisions for ourselves or anyone else. We must view danger with a calm and measured approach. Reasonable and fair assessments of danger can help us better navigate the individual realities that we do actually need to consider for safety for ourselves and our families.

The Size Instinct

Counting the deaths of children is not a job that anyone wishes to take. In order to find the best route for health care options for the greatest number of people, it must be done by someone. Author Hans Rosling tells of a time when he found himself counting dead children. He felt the need to better assess the risks to the district in which he was serving as a physician in Mozambique. His goal was to better determine how many child deaths could be avoided through better health options and education for the wider community.

His goal involved helping to prevent the need to come to the hospital in which he saw patients more directly. His experience included another physician who did not agree with the practices in which he chose to apply for the benefit of the patients who did make it to the hospital. Rosling sought to work under a wider spectrum of options for the greater good of a higher number of people. These ambitions offered a more preventative philosophy.

Rather than treat the dying as they reach the grave, Rosling sought to find ways in which their illness could be treated earlier and more effectively. His claim was that deaths that are not seen because they do not happen are lives that are saved. Preventative care is far less expensive and primarily involves education of the mothers, vaccinations, and basic medical considerations earlier in the discovery of an illness.

Medical care in nations of poverty must become something that is done with a wider range of focus. Focusing all of your attention for caring for the life of one may lead to the deaths of many others that could have been prevented via a wider scope of vision for the community as a whole. This does not mean that it should automatically become easy to 'look away' from the one life directly in front of a doctor. Neither option is easy, but one leads to many lives saved and one leads to saving the life of one that – now much progressed in an illness – may or may not live either way.

Numbers help us determine where help is most needed but they must not be the only factors that we consider when working to help others live happy and healthy lives. Hospitals have their place and need to be managed accordingly. However, on Levels 1 and 2, a good portion of the necessary medical procedures done to prevent disease and major illnesses is done outside of hospitals and within local communities with very little modern amenities. Educating the parents is key to preventing a great multitude of ailments and illnesses for all members of the family. An increase in child survival rates has not come from building structures for a few who have the means to access them. No. It is through local nurses and community action that families learn to spend their resources searching for clean water – not traveling to a building far away after diarrhea has begun. Hans Rosling states that on Levels 1 and 2 it is far more beneficial to seek the betterment of 'primary schools, nurse education, and vaccinations' than it is to build a large number of hospitals that many individuals may not even be able to reach.

Hans Rosling notes that the Size Instinct boils down to being able to compare and divide numbers. Always compare numbers and percentages with other numbers and percentages. Lone figures need something that offers an understanding of an incline or decrease in the situation. One figure by itself does not offer the opportunity to determine if a change has occurred or not. Hans Rosling reasons that the size of some health concerns becomes emphasized more than others because of media intervention.

Hans outlines the details of 31 deaths due to swine flu receiving greater media coverage than the deaths of more than 63,000 due to tuberculosis. Rosling presents what he calls the "80/20," in which he seeks out what is causing the largest portion of an issue and works to minimize the impact of that factor first. He applies this method to possibilities for global energy sources, budget matters, and the locations of the roughly 7 billion people residing on earth.

Western countries have experienced Level 4 lifestyles for quite some time, mostly without the company of Non-Western countries in the same category. As the nations of the world continue to make advancements, Western countries will begin to make up less and less of the world's overall wealth.

Dividing to get percentages helps us to better see what a society may be experiencing. How many children per school does a community have? Rates and percentages offer a more accurate view of a community than just using whole numbers of people and circumstances.

Hans Rosling explains an interaction with a world leader of India who states that figures relating to global emissions need to be assessed per person – not per single countries. It is not fair – or reasonable – to count per country due to the drastic difference in the population sizes of the nations of the world.

Enjoying this book so far?

We would like to ask you for a favor: would you be kind enough to leave a quick review for this book on Amazon? It would be greatly appreciated!

The Generalization Instinct

The instinct to generalize situations and people associated with various parts of the world is largely unconscious, but we still do it. This means that we may often find ourselves functioning under a false set of beliefs. In some form, generalizations help us create a framework for understanding the world around us. We may be asked to make a purchase. If the terms used for the items we are to buy are too unique we will not have an understanding of what is needed.

Generalizations have their place in society but can become overused causing us to assume that everyone in a particular clothing style may wish to cause harm to other individuals. The instinct to generalize anything and everything can cause us to hold an incorrect view of the world in which we live. Working to understand the difference between stereotypes and helpful generalizations that may express a particular need that a society retains can be a wonderful asset to businesses and investors. Knowing what basic needs a large population of individuals on Levels 2 and 3 may have can offer great insight for where investments might best be made.

Correctly generalizing the need for toothbrushes and the needs of menstruating females may better allow companies to market products they already manufacture. Rather than busting a mental sweat trying to remarket the same things over and over to Level 4 consumers, companies may want to consider selling their products in countries that are just beginning to have the means to purchase the items.

Hans Rosling recounts his experience with a family in Tunisia with an interesting housing situation. A bank in which to store funds to build their dream home was not available to them. Therefore, they were in the habit of purchasing individual bricks and supplies as they could afford them. They would attach them to the structure of their home as they were purchased.

To the outsider, this may offer a confusing and unfit scene. To them, it was the slow realization of a dream house – brick by brick, piece by piece. Similarly, a world leader is noted as having made regular observations as to whether or not grass has begun to grow over the homes resting in a state of mid-construction. The leader noted that if grass was not growing over the forming structures, then residents in his jurisdiction were likely doing fairly well.

Numbers help us form a method for understanding the world, but numbers alone must not be relied upon. The authors seek to help readers understand that a greater and more creative form of observation must also be utilized in order to more accurately understand whether or not a community is thriving or simply attempting to survive. Numbers are great, but what is behind them must also be understood.

Working to grasp how much the term 'majority' actually refers to in a particular situation can help investors and world leaders more accurately do their jobs. Examples that present vivid and dramatic circumstances may bring us to a false perception of the whole of something. Consider whether or not such matters may be an exception to the rule in any particular setting.

Assuming that people are idiots on the surface may leave us playing the role of the idiot. Just because someone makes a choice that does not make sense to us does not mean that it was not a choice that they should not have made. Perhaps their understanding of a situation comes from a perspective that is more closely united with their daily realities. Perhaps their decisions are in direct reflection to a situation they must manage that those living on Level 4 have never had to experience. Perhaps we can learn from basic solutions to problems that can more easily be solved from within the society in which they exist.

Dollar Street is a **website**[2] that Hans Rosling notes is the "brainchild" of Anna Rosling Rönnlund. The goal of this resource is to better help those who cannot travel or fully experience all that multiple global communities experience understand how other people really live. Anna's argument for the topic included that people will often not wish to leave the comforts of their own lives just to see what others experience.

Therefore, she proposed Dollar Street as a way for them to more accurately view the differences that are seen on each of the 4 Levels as described in the book. A dollar per month amount is shown with images and a brief summary of each family as presented across a number of income levels. The summaries include each family's setting, immediate goals, and what they value most in their home.

---

[2] https://www.gapminder.org/dollar-street/matrix

The Destiny Instinct

Short-sighted vision can lead to incredibly expensive mistakes. If a company is looking to market their products to a wider audience but their scope of vision is only as wide as it has always been they will lose much of their ability to grow. Automatically assuming that large portions of the world will not be interested in or able to afford your products may give your competitors the edge they need to gain a lead over you and your company.

A community's rules regarding sex and conversation have often hindered improvements to education regarding sexual health and family planning. In the same regard, religion has not always played as big of a role in stopping couples from using contraception as is often believed. The authors work to show that the number of children that a woman is likely to have in her lifetime is more directly related to the income level of her family. As income levels increase across whole nations, the number of births per woman that occur in that country tend to drop.

As mothers are more equipped and informed on how to safely raise their children, they are less likely to birth five or more children. According to the text, the average number of babies per woman was 2.5 in 2017 – across the globe. This is not to say that religion and personal beliefs do not have any impact on the number of children born to a family. However, these matters have far less of an impact on the *overall* numbers that are presented by data related to births worldwide.

The authors reason that extreme measures are not currently needed in order to control the population of the globe. Sexual education, family planning, and contraception are already doing that job for us. The steps that we are already doing have already begun to take effect. We just need to let these steps continue to be a part of public education and do the work that we have already directed them to do in our communities. The authors note that the number of births per year worldwide has already stopped increasing this, however, not mean that certain regions do not see increases and changes on a local level.

The same medicine that helps us to offer a better chance for reaching adulthood also helps with changes for a better life overall. As medicine improves and we are able to prevent more and more horrific diseases, the life expectancy of people everywhere also begins to improve. It is not uncommon to see relatives live into their 70's and the data supports this concept worldwide.

Today, it is not unrealistic to expect to see one's grandchildren get married. Such hopes were rarely seen prior to the last 200 or so years in world history. Again, the authors do not intend to say that no one ever lived past the age of 69. However, with the severity of wars, quantity of diseases, and lack of medical resources living past one's 30's was seen much less often prior to 1800 than it is today.

Philanthropic efforts to help those in poverty-ridden cultures should not be halted simply for the purpose of trying to control the human population. Instead, the authors argue that educating mothers living on low-income levels will, in time, actually help to decrease the number of births that a community sees. From this, regions that still retain a higher number of families with lower incomes can begin to see fewer and fewer child deaths, resulting in a higher and higher life expectancy.

Hans noted that simply making choices to benefit children who have not yet been born in the midst of children who are currently suffering due to extreme poverty was hard for him to watch. His argument includes that properly caring for and educating today's impoverished children is the best thing that we can do for children who will be born in the future. Helping these individuals now will better prepare the next generation.

Assuming that because data has always presented one type of figure or line on a chart does not mean that the same figure or line will always be seen. Mankind is a moving and dynamic species. To assume that its matters will always paint the same picture over and over again is shortsighted and foolhardy. Instead, we must always be ready to search out current data that better shows the inner-workings of our species.

Readers are encouraged to speak with members of the older generations and learn how drastically the world really has changed. Observe cultures and how they have changed as incomes have changed. Be ready to work within the framework of new information throughout the tasks of daily life.

The Single Perspective Instinct

Viewing life from one angle prevents us from absorbing all that may be gained by loving and enjoying something that we may not have expected. World leaders, Nobel laureates, and bank CEOs have the ability to get things wrong sometimes. If even the highly educated are still getting things wrong about matters of global development, health, and safety, what are members of society being taught regarding such important considerations?

Numbers help us determine what must be done and when progress has been made. Numbers alone, however, can easily provide us with a warped view of what those numbers actually mean. Hans relates to one community leader who has learned to look at the feet of his citizens during a time of marching to see how many of them are wearing shoes. This leader feels that if shoes are available to his people, then matters are not too dire at the time. This type of observation gives leaders a more colorful perception regarding any numbers that they may choose to consider for determining the health of their society.

Factfulness involves understanding that employing a single perspective can limit your ability to be creative. Instead of only employing a hammer in your work, the authors suggest getting a toolbox. Test your ideas against people who disagree with your perspective for the betterment of both sides. Be willing to have the skills of others complement your own field of expertise.

The Blame Instinct

As humans, we often have a hard time taking the blame for something. It is often easier to just say that someone we cannot see is responsible for the situation we are facing. Hans tells a story about one of his class sessions in which the students are lead to discover that their grandparents may unknowingly be responsible for undesirable situations in the world of pharmaceuticals due to the placement of their retirement funds. A circle of blame brings the students back to their own families. The text draws the reader to seek understanding for a situation prior to playing the blame game. Perhaps the blame is much closer to home than may initially be understood.

The text explains the history of what is called the "foreign disease." Syphilis was considered such a horrible skin disease that local communities had begun to feel that it was too terrible to have come from them. They began to call it after the name of neighboring countries when, in fact, the disease was quite widespread. The instinct to blame a "scapegoat" is noted as "core to human nature" by the authors. Would you name a disease after your own community?

Hans notes that his recommendation is not to seek to blame a particular person when things go wrong – but to look at the systems of a situation. He feels that we need to give positive credit to institutions and technology. In his observations, these two "unsung heroes" represent much of what humans have done for the betterment of all mankind. He recalls the time when his family "inaugurated" their first washing machine. His mother told him that the machine would wash their clothes and they could go to the library instead of having to wash them by hand. He notes, "in went the laundry, and out came the books." Hans expresses his gratitude for steel, power, and industry for giving him the time to read books.

The authors encourage that factfulness means that we should look for the cause of things instead of wasting time seeking a villain. We are better off looking for systems that work than merely honoring single heroes.

The Urgency Instinct

Resisting the urge to make quick decisions can help us save lives and heartache. Once again, Hans tells of a time when he worked as a physician in a rural community in extreme poverty. This time he makes a decision that causes deaths that he feels could have been prevented. His observation of the situation in retrospect was different than when he felt the need to make a decision quickly.

Hans felt that if he had only paused long enough to consider what closing a road may have meant for the members of that community, he may have acted differently. Of course, they would try to find another route. Had the road not been closed, multiple people would not have drowned needlessly on rickety boats trying to access the market to sell their goods. Hans khas ept this information close at heart for many years.

He notes that he spent many hours working to discover the reason behind a confusing disease. Yet, he spent less than a minute considering a roadblock that caused unnecessary deaths. A series of similar events with other people and other roadblocks due to Ebola outbreaks eventually helps to uncover a cycle of improper food preparation. Hans is able to use this information to help communities understand that, the root of a tropical tree, can be poisonous causing paralysis and other health concerns.

The reader is prompted to make immediate decisions regarding a response to having read the book. Then the true lesson is presented. Readers are reminded to understand that marketers use the human sense of urgency to sell their products all the time. Do you really need another stack of fancy dishes – or does the seller just want to feel that your current set is inferior so you will buy theirs?

The urgency for survival has its place in the world. If the building we are in is on fire, a healthy sense of the need to leave is beneficial. We must learn to control the urgency instinct whether or not the immediate danger is near us. Otherwise, we risk treating problems and situations that may not really exist.

The realities of global warming are real. They must be considered. However, in order to tell if what we are doing is working, we must seek the collection of regular data. Some of what mankind is doing to slow and stop its effects may have already begun to have some impact, but how can we tell for sure? How much do we really know about the tasks we spend our time on for the benefit of future generations?

Readers are encouraged to take small steps that matter. Recognize when something feels urgent and work to understand whether or not that is actually true. Factfulness includes remembering to breathe when important decisions must be made. It includes insisting on relevant and accurate data all the time. Trying to understand too much about the future may leave you with inaccurate information since the future is never fully knowable. Avoiding drastic action may be less dramatic but is noted as usually being more effective.

Factfulness in Practice

Thoughtfulness vs. Factfulness: What is the difference? The Rosling authors want for individuals on all income levels to have access to accurate and up to date information regarding world economies, changing populations, health, and the health of the globe, and the well-being of mankind as a species. In order for this to happen the education of the first willing parties must begin.

From that, we must work to help educate those who may not have ready access to the information and resources that would offer a more accurate worldview of matters as they are now. Readers are encouraged to recognize their direct role in helping others gain the knowledge that is now available through community action, Gapminder.com and its resources, and a more researched perspective of what is discovered as we live our daily lives.

The difference between a *just thoughtful observance* of any particular situation and what the authors *want to have happen* is this: when we take the time to observe the situations in life, we must do so in a manner that provides us with information that is true and relevant in all regards. We must make decisions using information that accurately reflects the situation under observation. Outdated perspectives and false worldviews have no place in a world that changes faster than people can finish their own education and have families of their own.

Factfulness Rules of Thumb

The Rosling authors present 10 Factfulness Rules of Thumb. In these concepts, we are given small phrases and identifying terminology to help us hold onto the principles of the book. Visual reminders of each topic discussed in the book are given to help the reader better visualize what has been learned.

1. Gap – Look for the majority.
2. Negativity – Expect bad news.
3. Straight Line – Lines might bend.
4. Fear – Calculate the risks.
5. Size – Get things in proportion.
6. Generalization – Question your categories.
7. Destiny – Slow change is still change.
8. Single – Get a toolbox.
9. Blame – Resist pointing your finger
10. Urgency – Take small steps.

Readers are encouraged to consider these concepts when making decisions for the betterment of their communities and families. Instead of remaining content with outdated information, we are directed to insist on accurate and relevant information. The questions presented in the book are meant to drive the general public to a better understanding of how we can grow with our world as it changes. Education and technology must be used to further gain understanding.

BACKGROUND INFORMATION ABOUT THE BOOK

Hans Rosling notes that in decades past his efforts to gain information and educate others regarding that information appalled him. Surveys, classroom interactions, and conference conversations led to a need to further provide global citizens with a more accurate picture of the state of matters worldwide. The result was a search for what the public really understood about the state of modern society.

From this, all three Rosling authors learned far more than might have been expected and encountered data that led them to understand that random guesses can offer a higher percentage of accuracy in comparison to what educated members of society might have guessed. Appalled and perplexed by their findings, the Rosling authors needed a way to provide the public with the results of their work.

The book's inception began out of the Rosling authors desire to educate the general public on matters they felt were important. World economics, rates of births and deaths, poverty, health, education, and climate change are all matters that need constant review in order to properly address related matters in large and small scales across the globe.

The book *Factfulness: Ten Reasons We're Wrong About the World- -and Why Things Are Better Than You Think* uses wit and humor to draw the reader into a better understanding of what global societies are actually facing. Instead of stressing and overdramatizing the needs of our global society, the authors want to teach people how to look for false perceptions, find a more accurate view of each situation as it is encountered, and then work to solve the problems that really do still exist without undermining the realities of poverty, disease, death, and harmful circumstances.

"Our joint work," Hans wrote, *"is finally being turned into an enjoyable text that will help a global audience to understand the world.³"*

BACKGROUND INFORMATION ABOUT THE AUTHORS

Although Hans Rosling was born in Uppsala, Sweden and later died there, he did not stay put there his entire life. Hans served as a physician internationally and in a number of low-income situations. As a TED speaker and well-known statistician, Hans sought to gather accurate data and then disperse his findings for the benefit and well-being of modern society. Hans also served as a Professor of International Health in Stockholm at the Karolinska Institute. Lifetime honors for Hans included finding his name on *Time*'s list of *The World's 100 Most Influential People: 2012*[4].

Hans was diagnosed with pancreatic cancer near the time of the book's beginning and died in 2013, leaving behind a legacy for others to have the right to an accurate worldview. After his death, co-authors Ola Rosling and Anna Rosling Rönnlund together took on the task of finalizing the work.

---

[3] Rosling, Hans. *Factfulness: Ten Reasons We're Wrong About the World--and Why Things Are Better Than You Think* (p. 258). Flatiron Books. Kindle Edition.
[4]
http://content.time.com/time/specials/packages/completelist/0,29569,2111975,00.html

Ola Rosling is the son of Hans Rosling. Ola has played an important role in the development of Trendalyzer. Trendalyzer is a software that is used to create visual images that help the public understand the data that is gathered by the Gapminder Foundation. The dynamics of the software allow for a current and usable data. Along with his wife Anna Rosling Rönnlund, Ola was honored with the *World Technology Award for Design* (2010).

Anna Rosling Rönnlund is the wife of Ola Rosling and daughter-in-law to Hans Rosling. Her creative and realistic nature plays very well to the nature of the research needed to develop the book and the data needed to publish accurate findings. Dollar Street was an alternative that she came up with to better help educate a wider base of people. Realizing that armchair travelers are more quantitative that actual travelers, Anna notes that a different method is needed to portray the 4 Levels of income that the book discusses.

All three Rosling authors have been awarded multiple awards for their efforts in collecting reliable data and working to educate the people of the world on their incredible findings.[5]

Ola recalls a strange accidental cell phone call that his father made while driving through traffic one day. During the call, a friend of Hans's could hear him singing the famous words of the song "My Way" along with Frank Sinatra. Ola notes that his father often had, "Two thoughts at the same time: concerned and full of joy."[6]

---

[5] https://www.gapminder.org/about-gapminder/awards/

It seems from the pages of this book that this would be a perspective that Hans would want others to consider. Take both sides of the coin and work to understand the whole coin. It is easier to make purchases that way.

---

[6] Rosling, Hans. *Factfulness: Ten Reasons We're Wrong About the World--and Why Things Are Better Than You Think* (p. 259). Flatiron Books. Kindle Edition.

Trivia Questions

(The correct answers are provided in footnotes.)

Who did Hans Rosling marry and how many children did they have?[7]

In what year does Hans fear that war is imminent with the arrival of a young Swedish air force pilot to the emergency room under his care?[8]

What type of weapons do muscly, angry village men raise at Hans as he attempts to study the consumption of cassava?[9]

What type of animal do the authors use to portray their perception of some of the results of their survey findings? [10]

According to the Rosling authors, what is the current PIN code of the world? [11]

---

[7] Agneta

[8] 1975

[9] Machetes

[10] Chimpanzees (specifically banana eating chimpanzees)

What did Hans Rosling notice that was hanging on the back of Sister Linda's (nun) door? [12]

Discussion Questions for Deeper Thinking

Going Off-Grid – What level might a person who chooses to live an off-grid lifestyle be placed? The book does not specifically state how this type of lifestyle might be addressed by the 4 Levels. If someone has the ability to purchase a washing machine but does not wish to do so, does that person automatically jump back down a few levels?

Individuals may *choose* to live under more basic living conditions for the purpose of minimizing their global footprint, personal enjoyment, or their families health. Might such a decision have been generated – at least in part – due to a view of global matters that are less than accurate?

On what level do you think the authors might put a modernized *indoor* composting toilet? If running water is an amenity found first on Level 3, then does that make an individual who *chooses* not to run water into their dwelling for environmental beliefs automatically fall back down to Level 2?

[11] 1-1-1-4

[12] Condoms

How much impact do you think the Rosling authors feel that money alone has to do with the choices that people make regarding their lifestyle? What if a family can technically afford certain items but *chooses* not to own them for personal or religious reasons – even in spite of their updated knowledge as provided by the text and new resources? On what level might the Rosling authors say such a family lived? Do you think the 4 Levels are only formed around what can be afforded by the income available to that family? What other considerations do the authors use to create the levels as described?

Public Education – Why is education such an important factor in how the individuals found on each level are able to jump – almost in single generations – from one level to the next? What educational choices can you make today to help you maintain an accurate understanding of matters in your current local community?

What story or fact struck you as most important for forming an even more up to date worldview? Is this concept being taught in educational institutions in your area? What might you be able to do to help make this happen on your end of Dollar Street?

How did you do on the Gapminder Test? Did you write down your answers to help you more accurately reflect your own current knowledge? Do you think that the world is getting better? Will you share your learnings with other community members? Who can you work with to help provide young generations with a hunger for accurate information? Who might be near you now that would most benefit from having interacted with Dollar Street and Gapminder?

CONCLUSION

Thank you for reading this book!

If you enjoyed the book, we would appreciate it if you could post a review of it on Amazon!

As a way of thanking you for purchasing *this* book, we would like to give you another book as a gift: *Stoicism: The Art of Living a Modern Stoic and Happy Life Now.*

If you would like a copy, please visit:

http://NoscoPublishing.com/offer/

Regards,

Nosco Publishing

Made in the USA
Middletown, DE
30 October 2018